Belief

or

Nonbelief?

Belief
or
Nonbelief?

A Confrontation

Umberto Eco

Cardinal Carlo Maria Martini

Translated from the Italian by
Minna Proctor

Introduction by Harvey Cox

Arcade Publishing • *New York*

FIRST ENGLISH-LANGUAGE EDITION

Originally published in Italian under the title *In cosa crede chi non
crede?* English-language edition arranged through the mediation of
Eulama Literary Agency.

ISBN 1-55970-497-7
Library of Congress Catalog Card Number 99-59727
Library of Congress Cataloging-in-Publication information is
available.

Published in the United States by Arcade Publishing, Inc.,
New York
Distributed by Time Warner Trade Publishing

Visit our Web site at www.arcadepub.com

10   9   8   7   6   5   4   3   2   1

Designed by API

BP

PRINTED IN THE UNITED STATES OF AMERICA

Contents

Belief

or

Nonbelief?

Introduction

by Harvey Cox

When the Italian newspaper *La Correra de la Serra* invited novelist-scholar Umberto Eco and bishop-scholar Carlo Maria Martini to engage in an exchange of views on its pages, the editors had obviously hit on a fresh and imaginative idea. But I doubt they could possibly have foreseen how brilliant the result of their conception would turn out to be. The Eco-Martini correspondence lifts the possibility of intelligent conversation on religion to a new level. It proves that the partners in such a discussion can probe and challenge and still remain respectful, even congenial. These letters are now being translated into a number of languages and will appear all over the world. It is all for the good. For American readers, it

1

might be helpful to know a bit more about the participants in the argument.

In Eco's labyrinthine novel *Foucault's Pendulum*, one character says to another, "I was born in Milan, but my family came from Val d'Aosta."

"Nonsense," the other replies, "You can always tell a genuine Piedmontese immediately by his skepticism."

"I'm a skeptic," says the first.

"No," replies his interlocutor, "you're only incredulous, a doubter, and that's different."

The reader has to wait a few more pages for Eco to pick up this twisted thread. But he does. And what he says might have served as a foreword to this remarkable correspondence.

✓   Not that the incredulous person doesn't believe in anything. It's just that he doesn't believe in everything. Or he believes in one thing at a time. He believes in one thing only if it somehow follows from the first thing. He is nearsighted and methodical, avoiding wide horizons. If two things don't fit, but you believe both of them, thinking that somehow, hidden, there must be a third thing that connects them, that's credulity.

Umberto Eco was born in 1932 in Alessandria, in the Piedmont area of Italy. Before becoming a renowned scholar in the field of semiotics (the branch of philosophy dealing with signs and symbols), he studied the aesthetic theories of the Middle Ages. At the University of Turin he wrote his thesis on the aesthetics of Thomas Aquinas. He is now professor of semiotics at the University of Bologna. By his own account Eco was a practicing Catholic until the age of twenty-two. But he is not an angry, antireligious ex-Catholic. He even seems at times to speak about his lost faith with a hint of regret, and suggests that the solid sense of morality that underlies his life and his writing may well have derived from his earlier Catholic formation. That formation is highly evident, some might even say on display, in his writing. His novel *Foucault's Pendulum* makes extensive references to the medieval Templars and the *Corpus Hermeticum*. And who can forget the Latin citations, like the illuminated letters that embellish old hand-copied biblical texts, that

3

garland each chapter heading in *The Name of the Rose*? If they were used by other writers, the average reader might have found these quotations a bit ostentatious. But, for some reason, we let Eco get away with them. Maybe because the luster of the whole novel and his evident command of European religious history demonstrate that he is not faking. He can write with equal ease about philosophy and aesthetics, Thomas Aquinas and James Joyce, computers and the Albigenses. And this is what makes him such a fascinating — and, I would say, from an American perspective — enviable collaborator in this conversation. Would that we American religionists had minds like his to engage with in this country, thinkers who know what they are talking about when they disagree with theologians, interlocutors who are incredulous but not principled skeptics. Would that we had dialogue partners who, as Eco himself puts it, may not themselves believe in God, but realize how arrogant it would be to declare, for this reason, that God does not exist. Eco is one of those mature sages who is not interested in refuting religious believers but in illu-

4

minating genuine differences and finding common ground.

In his first letter to Martini, Eco suggests that they both "aim high." They do. There are no rhetorical gambits, no cheap shots. When they struggle with famously controversial questions, like abortion and women's ordination, they do not trample the familiar ground but delve into the underlying paradigms and historical processes that inform today's arguments. In his own terms, Eco is a man marked by a restless incredulity, not a closed skepticism.

Carlo Maria Martini is no more interested in refuting nonbelievers than Eco is in tripping up Christians. He is also a relentless searcher for common ground. I once heard him tell a large crowd of listeners that when he speaks about "believers" and "nonbelievers," he does not have two different groups of people in mind. He says he means, rather, that in all of us there is something of the believer and something of the nonbeliever, and this, he added, "is true of this bishop as well." It is unusual to find a prominent agnostic intellectual, like Eco, who is so open to the deepest questions of faith. It is also unusual to find a prince of the Church who is so open to the serious questions of a thoughtful agnostic.

Martini was born in Turin in 1927 and — like his correspondent — studied philosophy and theology. But then he traveled in a different direction. He was ordained to the priesthood in 1952 and became a member of the Society of Jesus. Beginning in 1978 he served as the Rettore Magnifico (rector) of the Gregorian University in Rome, the most prestigious Roman Catholic university in the world. For the past twenty years he has been the Archbishop of Milan. In December 1979 Pope John Paul II named him a cardinal. A broadly, humanely educated man, Martini is a respected scholar of the New Testament. His name appears as one of the editors of the most widely used critical edition of the Greek New Testament. In addition to his scholarly works he is a highly prolific writer of spiritual books for laypeople. He is also one of the leading ecumenical churchmen of Europe and takes special interest in the relations of Christians to Jews. Although he himself dismisses the possibility out of hand, Martini has been spoken of as a possible future pontiff.

A few years ago I learned from personal observation how genuine Martini's interest in frank and unfettered dialogue is. Martini's Milan is a city redolent with the memories of Saint Ambrose (who was its bishop) and Saint Augustine (who was baptized there), and remembered as the diocese headed by Giovanni Cardinal Montini before he became Pope Paul VI. Every year in this historic metropolis, Martini stages an open conversation in a huge downtown auditorium. He calls it the Cattedra dei Non Credenti (Lecture Series for Nonbelievers), and he invites both religious participants and nonbelievers to exchange views on a topic of pressing interest to both. It has come to be an immensely popular event, drawing tens of thousands of Milanese for several evenings away from their towering glass offices and throbbing nightclubs. Tickets are free but one must request them, and they are always in short supply. The year I participated priests and laypeople, nuns and fashion models, scholars, bankers, and politicians — including the mayors of the four largest cities in Italy — came together to discuss "The City: Blessing or Curse?" Cardinal Martini himself, in splendid vestments, presided over the meetings and offered his own comments. Milan is a busy hub; it is both the high-style and high-finance capital of Italy. The energetic Milanese work hard and play even harder. But despite the film openings, theatrical productions, concerts, and numerous art exhibits going on in the city at the same time, it was clear that Martini's gathering was the event no one wanted to miss. More than two thousand crowded into a huge auditorium to attend. It was "the open church" at its best, a demonstration not only of what the church should be but what, at times, it already is. Its only limitation was that it took place in one city and in one country. But could what happened during those weeks in Milan become more general? Might it be a sign of things to come? Was it only exceptional, or does it represent the kind of format that could easily be multiplied a hundred-fold? Would it work, for example, in America?

I have frequently pondered these questions since my return from Milan. But I have still not arrived at an answer. On the one hand, sociologists assert that in terms of religiousness — as measured by standard criteria — the United States is far more pious than

8

any country in Europe (with the possible exceptions of Ireland and Poland). Surveys show that church attendance is higher, and more people answer pollsters affirmatively on such questions as whether they believe in God or whether they think religion should play an important role in life. But is American religiosity like the famous lake that is a thousand miles wide and one inch deep? Would urban Americans in large numbers forgo an evening at the theater (or in front of a flickering blue screen) to listen to religious and secular practitioners, scholars and creative writers, exchanging views on a theme of common topical import? Is there an audience, or even a potential audience, for such a conversation in America?

We may have the opportunity to give at least a partial answer to this question. The test case is the volume the reader now holds in his or her hands. This exchange of letters between Martini and Eco is sophisticated, demanding, thorough, and engaging. When I first read it, it reminded me at times of Louis Malle's film *My Dinner With Andre*, which was released in the early 1980s. That film boldly depicted nothing more than a fascinating conversation between two old friends over a pleasant meal, an evening during which they touch on a variety of topics for nearly two hours. There are no shootings, no sex scenes, and no car chases. It was reported that the producers wondered whether anyone would pay to see it. But people did, and in sufficiently large numbers to make it a reasonable success. It was both entertaining and thought provoking. It sent audiences home with a renewed faith in the sheer possibility of human conversation. The Eco-Martini correspondence is a little like that. It presupposes — in fact, demands — a reader who would not be satisfied with the snide thrusts and clever parries that characterize those "talking heads" television programs that present themselves as intellectual discussions. But the reward for reading these letters will be twofold: they demonstrate not only that conversation is still viable and valuable, but that respectful disagreement on very basic issues is still possible.

But why should we have to be convinced that such a classic form of human communication is not only still attractive but possibly even desperately needed? How have we fallen into such noisy muteness? And why is religion such a daunting thing to talk about that we either tiptoe around it or resort to shrieking? I do not believe this dismal situation is all the fault of the media. The problem is also to be found in the nature of American religiousness itself. It is a problem that, paradoxically, is a result of the same quality that might well be the great strength of American religion, namely its dizzying variety. If we can make the distinction that Eco's character in *Foucault's Pendulum* does between skepticism and incredulity, there may not be much of a place for the total skeptic in one of our multitudinous American denominations. Yet there is certainly ample room for the incredulous. If Mormonism, Christian Science, Lubavitcher Judaism, and the various strains of Protestant fundamentalism require one to believe quite a list of things, there are always liberal Congregationalism, Reform Judaism, Ethical Culture, and, above all, Unitarianism to accommodate various degrees of incredulity. Furthermore, unlike in Europe where religion almost always took the side of the establishment in social conflicts, in America it has just as often been a progressive force. This is the land where Baptists and Congregationalists helped light the fires of the American Revolution, preachers took to the barricades for abolition, and clergy marched against segregation and the Vietnam War. Therefore, America never developed the rabid political anticlericalism of Europe, so it was hard, on this side of the Atlantic, for critics of religion to portray religion as the bulwark of reaction.

The result of all this is that the critics of American religion have never had enough opportunity to sharpen their lances. Take, for example, our bewildering plethora of religious possibilities. They provide an elusive target. Whenever the skeptics lunge, instead of clashing against a shield or receiving a sharp counterblow, their spears sink into a porous sponge of spiritual possibilities. Instead of a counterargument they may just as often be offered a membership application, a pledge card, and a cup of coffee. All this makes for a nice atmosphere, but it hardly raises the intellectual level of the conversation between believers and nonbelievers. Nor does it provide much for those who, like Martini and many of the rest of us, find ourselves divided or somewhere in between. One wonders occasionally whatever happened to the once audacious voices of American atheism like those of Thomas Paine and Robert Ingersoll. The best we have done in recent years was the late lamented Madalyn Murray O'Hair, that stalwart citizen who introduced the first successful legal complaint against school prayer. But O'Hair was hardly a credible tribune for nonbelievers. Her short, tumultuous public career succeeded mainly in demonstrating that in these matters stridency is no substitute for thoughtfulness.

Predictably, the weakness of serious questioning of religious faith in America has had the result of rendering religion's intellectual defenders listless and sedentary. Our theologians spend more time sorting out the sometimes cordial but also sometimes troubled relations among our many faith groupings than in exploring the underlying issue of faith itself. Ms. O'Hair never really made a very good case against religion. She just did not want the government to make her children pray in school, something on which —ironically — many religious people agreed with her. Our newspapers become more exercised over whether Southern

Baptists should try to convert Jews than on whether either Christianity or Judaism can make a plausible case to the postmodern mind. Do we need a rebirth of what theologians call "polemics" and "apologetics"? I think so, but if it ever comes, I hope and pray it will be of the elegant, informed, and truly empathetic quality demonstrated in this epistolary exchange.

Reading this book left me wanting more. Martini and Eco could easily have gone on to a whole range of other topics. Perhaps the success this collection has found will inspire them to do so. Also, it is largely the professor-novelist who is posing the questions and the scholarly bishop who is trying to understand and respond. Only in the latter part does the bishop suggest a question to the novelist, and it is a terribly important one. He asks with genuine curiosity how people who do not believe in God, or in some transcendent source of meaning and value, can escape falling into the kind of relativism that in recent years has teetered so close to nihilism. I believe the answer Eco gives is an excellent one, but I am still wondering how Martini would have responded. Instead, perhaps intentionally, the reader is left to sort this out without any help from the friendly protagonists.

Once, sitting in his garden, the young Augustine, who was eventually baptized in what is now Martini's Milan, and only much later became a saint, heard a voice that said, "Pick up, and read." I leave the reader of this splendid volume with the same counsel.

Secular Obsession with the New Apocalypse

Dear Carlo Maria Martini,

I hope you won't think me disrespectful for addressing you by the name you bear, without reference to the robe you wear. Take it as an act of homage and of prudence. Homage, because I've always been struck by the way the French avoid using reductive designations such as Doctor, Your Eminence, or Minister when they interview a writer, an artist, a political figure. There are people whose intellectual capital comes from the name they sign their ideas with. This is how the French address someone whose own name is his principal title: *"Dites-moi,* Jacques Maritain"; *"Dites-moi,* Claude Lévi-Strauss." Using a person's name is a way of acknowledging an authority that he would have had even if he had he not become an ambassador or a member of the French Academy. If I were to address Saint Augustine (and again you shouldn't mistake the extravagance of my example for irreverence), I would not call him "lord bishop of Hippo" (because there were other lord bishops of Hippo who came after Saint Augustine), I'd call him "Augustine of Tagaste."

Act of prudence, I also said. Indeed, what has been asked of the two of us could prove awkward — an exchange of opinions between a layman and a cardinal. It might appear that the point is for the layman to solicit opinions from the cardinal in his role as a prince of the Church and a shepherd of souls. Such a thing would constitute an injustice, to the one appealed to as well as to his listener. Better that we carry out this dialogue the way the newspaper that brought us together intended — an exchange of ideas between free men. What's more, by addressing you this way, I mean to underscore the fact that you are considered a leader of intellectual and moral life, even by those readers who are not committed to any belief or teaching other than that of reason.

Having resolved the problems of etiquette, we are left with those of ethics. I believe this is what we should be primarily concerning ourselves with during the course of our dialogue, as the goal is to find some points of commonality between the Catholic and secular worlds (and I wouldn't think it realistic in these pages to open a debate on the *filioque*). But even here, as I am called on to make the first move (always the most awkward), I don't think we need to focus on the immediate questions of the day — which may be where our positions would most immediately be too divergent. Better to aim high, and only touch on subjects that, while topical, have their roots far enough back in history, and have been a source of fascination, fear, and hope for all members of the human family over the course of the last two millennia.

I've uttered the key word. We are indeed at the end of the second millennium; and I do hope it is still politically correct in Europe to use a calendar based on an event that has had — and even an adherent of another religion, or of no religion, may allow me this — a profound influence on the history of our planet. The approach of this terminal date can't help but evoke an image that has dominated twenty centuries of thought: the Apocalypse.

Vulgate history teaches us that the final years of the first millennium were obsessed by the notion of the end of time. It's true that historians have already branded as legend the notorious "horrors of the year 1000," the vision of hordes of howling people waiting for a new dawn that would never come. But historians also point out that the notion of the end preceded that fatal day by some centuries and, what's even more curious, persisted *after* it, too. From there ensued the various millenarianisms of the second millennium, which did not grow only out of religious movements, orthodox or heretical as the case may be, but also — because by now we tend to classify many political and social movements as forms of millenarianism — out of secular, even atheist, movements whose purpose, racing headlong toward the end of time, was not to reach the Kingdom of God but to realize a new Kingdom on Earth.

The Revelation of St. John is a terrifying, conflicted book, as are the apocryphal apocalyptic sequels associated with it — apocryphal according to the canon; authentic in the effects, passions, terrors, and movements they have given rise to. Revelation can be read as a promise, but also as an announcement of an end, and thus gets rewritten at every step, even by those who have never read it, as we await 2000. No more the seven trumpets, the hailstorm, the sea turned to blood, stars falling from the sky, horses rising in a cloud of smoke from the deepest abyss, the armies of Gog and Magog, the Beast emerging from the sea. In their place: the uncontrolled and uncontrollable proliferation of nuclear waste; acid rain; the disappearing Amazon; the hole in the ozone; the migrating disinherited masses knocking, often with violence, at the doors of prosperity; the hunger of entire continents; new, incurable pestilence; the selfish destruction of the soil; global warming; melting glaciers; the construction of our own clones through genetic engineering; and, according to mystical principles of ecology, the necessary suicide of humanity itself, which must perish in order to rescue those species it has already almost obliterated — Mother Earth, denatured and suffocating.

We are living out (albeit with that degree

of apathy to which new modes of mass communication have accustomed us) our own fears about the end. One could even say that we live our fear in the spirit of *bibamus, edamus, cras moriemur* [eat, drink, for tomorrow we die], celebrating the end of ideology and solidarity in a whirlwind of irresponsible consumerism. In this way, each one of us flirts with the specter of the apocalypse, exorcising it; the more one unconsciously fears it the more one exorcises, projecting it onto the screen in the form of bloody spectacle, hoping in this way to render it unreal. But the power of specter lies precisely in its unreality.

I'd be willing to bet that the notion of the end of time is more common today in the secular world than in the Christian. The Christian world makes it the object of meditation, but acts as if it may be projected into a dimension not measured by calendars. The secular world pretends to ignore the end of time, but is fundamentally obsessed by it. This is not a paradox, but a repetition of what transpired in the first thousand years of history.

I do not want to linger on exegetical questions that you are more familiar with than I am, but I will remind readers that the idea of the end of time comes out of one of the most ambiguous passages of John's text, chapter 20, which gives us the following "scenario": With the Incarnation and the Redemption, Satan is imprisoned, but *after one thousand years* will return, and that is when the final battle between the forces of good and evil occurs, crowned by the return of Christ and the Last Judgment. John, unambiguously, speaks of a thousand years. But some of the Church Fathers already explained that a thousand years for the Lord can mean one day, or one day can last a thousand years, and so this calculation should not be interpreted literally. Augustine's interpretation of that passage is in keeping with a "spiritual" reading. The millennium or the promise of the Kingdom of God are not historical but mystical events, and Armageddon is not of this earth. This is not to deny that one day history may complete itself, and Christ descend to judge the living and the dead, but the emphasis is not on the *end* of the centuries but on their *passing*, dominated by the notion (one of regularity, not of history's expiration) of Parousia, the Second Coming.

This approach, which isn't only

Augustine's but also the Church Fathers' as a whole, casts History as a journey forward — a notion alien to the pagan world. Even Hegel and Marx are indebted to this fundamental idea, which Pierre Teilhard de Chardin pursued. Christianity invented History, and it is in fact a modern incarnation of the Antichrist that denounces History as a disease. It's possible that secular historicism has understood history as infinitely perfectible — so that tomorrow we improve upon today, always and without reservation, and so that in the course of the same history God reconstitutes himself and in a manner of speaking educates and enriches himself. But the entire secular world is not of the ideological view that through history we understand how to look at the regression and folly of history itself. There is, nonetheless, an originally Christian vision of history whenever the signpost of Hope on this road is followed. The simple knowledge of how to judge history and its horrors is fundamentally Christian, whether the speaker is Emmanuel Mounier on tragic optimism or Gramsci on pessimism of reason and optimism of will.

I suspect desperate millennialism will

occur whenever the end of time is seen as inevitable, and hope gives way to a celebration of the end of history, or to a plea for a return to a timeless and archaic Tradition that no act of will and no reflection — I don't say rational, but reasonable — could ever enrich. From this is born the gnostic heresy (the secular versions of it, too) whereby the world and history are the fruits of error, and only by destroying both can the elect few redeem God himself. Various superman ideologies are also born from this, whereby only the members of a privileged race or sect will be able to celebrate their blazing holocaust on the miserable stage of the world and its history.

Only by having a sense of history's trajectory (even if one does not believe in Parousia) can one love earthly reality and believe — with charity — that there is still room for Hope.

Is there a notion of hope (and of our responsibility to the future) that could be shared by believers and nonbelievers? What can it be based on now? Does an idea of the end, one that does not imply disinterest in the future but rather a constant examination of the errors of the past, have a critical function?

If not, it would be perfectly all right to accept the approach of the end, even without thinking about it, sitting in front of our TV screens (in the shelter of our electronic fortifications), waiting for someone to *entertain us* while meantime things go however they go. And to hell with what will come.

Umberto Eco

Hope Puts an End to "The End"

Dear Umberto Eco,

I am in complete agreement. You address me by my birth name and I shall do likewise. The Gospels are not altogether benevolent where titles are concerned. ("But you are not to be called rabbi. . . . And call no man your father on earth. . . . And you are not to be called masters." Matthew 23:8–10.) As you say, this way it is even clearer that ours is an exchange of ideas made freely, without plaster casts and role involvements. To be fruitful, it is important that our exchange be frank as we focus on common concerns and clarify the differences, getting to the substance of what truly distinguishes us from each other.

I also agree about "aiming a bit high" in our first dialogue.

Ethical issues are certainly among our most pressing concerns. But the matters of the day that most strongly strike public opinion (I'm referring particularly to those involving bioethics) are often "frontline" events, which we first have to understand from the scientific viewpoint before we rush to moral judgments on which we may easily disagree. It is important for us first to put into focus the broad horizons between which our judgments are being formed. From there, it will be apparent why practical valuations can be in such opposition.

You've raised the subject of hope and with it the future of mankind at the time of the second millennium. You evoke those apocalyptic images that were said to make the multitudes tremble at the end of the first millennium. Even if it isn't true, it is apt, because people do fear the future. Millenarianisms have been constantly reproducing themselves throughout the centuries, in parochial forms as well as in those implicit cataclysmic beliefs that have so profoundly animated the major utopian movements. Today ecological threats, even more upsetting because they are scientifically based, take the place of the phantasms of the past.

What does Revelation, the final book of the New Testament, have to do with all this? Can the book truly be characterized as a repository of terrifying imagery that evokes a tragic and imminent end? Despite the similarities between much of John's Revelation and numerous other apocalyptic writings of those centuries, the key to reading is different. It must be read in the context of the New Testament, in which Revelation was (not without resistance) incorporated.

Let me try to explain myself. The dominant theme of apocalyptic stories is usually a flight from the present to a refuge in a future that, upsetting the existing structures of the world, forces upon it a definitive value system that conforms to the hopes and expectations of the person writing the book. Always in the background of apocalyptic literature are groups of people suffering from religious, social, and political oppression who, not seeing any solution in direct action, project themselves into a time when cosmic forces will fall upon the earth and defeat their enemies for them. In this sense, it must be said that in every apocalypse there is a heavy utopian freight, a massive reserve of hope, but coupled with woeful resignation in the present.

One can, perhaps, find something similar behind individual documents that became part of Revelation as we know it today. But when read from a Christian perspective, in the light of the Gospels, the book's emphasis and meaning are different. It is not a projection of frustration with the present, but rather the prolongation of an experience of fullness — in other words, "salvation," as it was construed by the early church. There isn't now, nor will there be, a power human or satanic that can challenge the hope of believers.

In this sense, I am in agreement with you when you say that today preoccupation with the end of time is more typical of the secular world than the Christian world.

At one point the Christian world was also overcome by apocalyptic anxiety, having to do, in part, with obscure verses in Revelation 20: "And he seized the dragon, that ancient serpent, who is the Devil and Satan, and bound him for a thousand years. . . . Also I saw the souls of those who had been beheaded. . . . They came to life, and reigned with Christ a thousand years." A current of ancient tradition interpreted these verses to the letter, whereas other similar, literal millennialisms have never won legitimacy in the broader Church. Rather, a symbolic reading of the text has prevailed. In the above passage and in others in Revelation we again find a projection into the future of the victory of those first Christians who were able to survive their present thanks to their capacity for hope.

History has always been seen most clearly as a journey toward something beyond itself and not immanent. Such a view might be expressed as a triad of beliefs: 1) history has a meaning, a direction, and is not a heap of absurd, vain facts; 2) this meaning is not purely immanent, but extends beyond itself, and thus is not a matter for calculation but rather for hope; 3) this vision does not extenuate but solidifies the meaning of contingent events into an ethical locus in which the metahistorical future of the human adventure is determined.

Up to this point it would seem that we have both been basically saying the same thing, though with different emphases and a different set of references. I'm pleased we agree that history has "meaning" and (to cite your own words) that one can "love earthly reality and believe — with charity — that there is still room for Hope."

The more difficult question is whether there is a "notion" of hope (and of our responsibility to the future) which is common to both believers and nonbelievers. In some way, hope has to exist in practice, because believers and nonbelievers can be seen living together in this moment, giving it meaning and involving themselves with commitment. This is particularly apparent when we see someone who, in the pursuit of higher values, puts himself willingly in harm's way, even when there is no promise of reward. Thoughtful, responsible believers and nonbelievers adhere to a profound sense of *būmus*, of humanity, although they don't necessarily give it the same name. In the drama of the moment, there are more important things than names, and when defending or promoting essential human values it's not always worthwhile to quibble over a *quaestio de nomine*, over semantics.

For one who believes, especially for a Catholic, it is nonetheless evident that the names of things do have importance, because a name is not an arbitrary thing, but rather the product of an act of intelligence and comprehension that, when shared with someone else, also brings the recognition, however theoretical, of shared values. There is still a long road ahead of us, I believe, a road that calls for our mutual intelligence and courage to analyze the simple things. How often does Jesus say in the Gospels: "He who has ears to hear, let him hear." "Do you not perceive yet, not understand?" (Mark 4:9, 8:17, etc.). He's not appealing to philosophical theories or to disputes between various schools of thought but to the intelligence given each of us to orient ourselves and to understand the meaning of events. Every tiny step toward understanding the great simple things means progress toward sharing the reasons why we hope.

I am also struck by this provocation at the end of your letter: "Does an idea of the end, one that does not imply disinterest in the future but rather a constant examination of the errors of the past, have a critical function?"

I do not believe that in itself the notion of an imminent end provides us with the critical tools to evaluate what has been. If anything, the notion gives rise to fear, dread, self-recrimination, or flight toward an "alternative" future — precisely what we find in apocalyptic literature.

For a notion of the end to make us as aware of the future as we are of the past, as something to be reflected on in a critical way, this end must be an End, with the character of an ultimate declaration of value, illuminating our endeavors in the present and endowing them with significance. If the present has meaning in relation to a recognizable and estimable value, which I can anticipate with acts of intelligence and responsible choice, this allows me to reflect on the mistakes of the past without pain. I know I am on a journey. I glimpse something of the destination, at least in its essential values. I know it is up to me to correct myself and to better myself. Experience shows that someone with no regrets is someone with no inner inkling that he can do better. He cannot recognize his mistakes and remains attached to them, because he can't see anything better ahead

34

and so asks himself why he should give up what he has.

All I've written here seems like a set of variations on that word "Hope," which I perhaps never would have dared to write with a ✓ capital H had you not done so first. No, it's not yet time to intoxicate oneself on electronic images while waiting for the end. We still have much to do together.

Carlo Maria Martini

When Does Human Life Begin?

Dear Carlo Maria Martini,

According to the schedule we have agreed to, it is time for us to continue our conversation. The goal of this letter exchange is to identify common ground between lay people and Catholics (and I remind readers that you are participating as a believer and a man of culture, not in the robe of a prince of the Church). I have been wondering, however, if we should be limiting our discussion to include only what beliefs we have in common. Is it worthwhile for us to ask each other what we think about capital punishment or genocide, for example, only to discover the we agree profoundly on these topics and the values associated with them? For this to be a true dialogue, we should be exploring the subjects on which there is no consensus. Yet that's still not enough. A layperson does not believe in the Holy Spirit and a Catholic obviously does, for example, but that does not occasion a lack of understanding, just a mutual respect for our personal beliefs. The critical moment occurs when from disagreement is born a deeper conflict and incomprehension that can be translated into political and social agendas.

One such conflict is right-to-life versus existing abortion legislation.

Confronting a problem of this scope calls for putting one's cards on the table, and avoiding ambiguity. He who asks the question should clarify his own perspective as well as what he expects from the respondent. Hence, my first clarification: I have never been in the situation of having a woman tell me she is pregnant by me, and put the question to me as to whether to abort or to consent to her wish to abort. Had it ever happened, I would have done everything possible to persuade her to grant life to that being, whatever the price. The birth of a baby is a marvelous thing, a natural miracle that we must accept. That said, I don't feel I have the right to impose my own ethical position (my emotional disposition, my intellectual persuasion) on anyone. I believe there are terrible moments about which neither you nor I know very much (which is why I'll refrain from drawing hypothetical comparisons), when a woman has the right to make an autonomous decision about her body, her feelings, her future.

Nonetheless, there are those people who appeal to the right to life. If we cannot permit someone to kill another person, nor even to kill himself (I won't embroil myself in a debate about self-defense), we likewise cannot allow someone to halt the course of a life begun.

So we come to my second clarification: it would be inappropriate of me to ask you to express your opinion or restate the teachings of the Church. Instead, I am inviting you to offer your own reflections in relation to current doctrine on the subject. When the banner of Life is waved, it can't but move the spirit — especially of nonbelievers, however "pietistic" their atheism, because for those who do not believe in anything supernatural the idea of Life, the feeling of Life, provides the only value, the only source of a possible

38

ethical system. Despite that, there is no more elusive, nuanced, or, as today's logicians are wont to say, "fuzzy" concept. As the ancient Greeks knew, life is not recognized exclusively from the appearance of intellectual spirit, but also from the manifestation of sensory, even vegetative spirit. Nowadays, for example, there are "radical ecologists" who believe that Mother Earth with her mountains and volcanoes has a life unto herself, and who speculate the human race might have to disappear in order to ensure the survival of the planet it threatens. There are vegetarians, who sacrifice vegetable life to preserve animal life, and oriental ascetics who cover their mouths, so as not to swallow and kill invisible microorganisms.

At a recent conference, the African anthropologist Harris Memel-Fote noted that the typical attitude of the Western world is *cosmophagic* (a beautiful term: we have always tended to devour the universe). Now we should be open (and some societies already are) to some form of *negotiation*: between what mankind can do to nature in order to survive, and what it shouldn't do so that nature will survive. When negotiation occurs it's because there are still no fixed rules; one negotiates to establish them. I believe that, with the exception of certain extremist positions, we are constantly negotiating (more often with our emotions than our intellect) our concept of respect for life.

Most of us would be horrified at the idea of slaughtering a pig, but happily eat ham. I would never squash a caterpillar in the park, but am merciless when it comes to mosquitoes. I discriminate between bees and wasps (both constitute a threat, but I recognize virtues in the former that I don't in the latter). You could argue that while our perception of vegetable and animal life is nuanced, our perception of human life isn't. Yet this is a problem that has troubled theologians and philosophers for centuries. If, by chance, a properly trained or genetically manipulated monkey should show that it could type reasonable sentences into a computer, engaging in a dialogue, demonstrating affection, memory, the ability to solve mathematical problems, reactivity to logical principles of identity and perception of the Other — would we then consider it to be almost human? Would we grant it civil rights?

Because it thinks and loves? Yet we don't necessarily consider everything that loves to be human; in fact, we kill animals even though we know the mother "loves" her own offspring.

When does human life begin? Are there (today, never mind the customs of the Spartans) any nonbelievers who would affirm that a being is human only after his culture has initiated him into humanity, granting him language and articulated thought (which according to St. Thomas were external accidents that allowed us to infer the presence of rationality — one of the defining aspects of human nature), and who would condone the murder of a newborn because, in point of fact, he is only an "infant"? I think not. Everyone considers the newborn still attached to the umbilical cord to be a human being. But how far back do we go from there? If life and humanity already exist in the seed (in our genetic makeup, even), then is the wasting of semen a crime equal to homicide? The indulgent confessor of a tempted teenager wouldn't say that, and neither do the Scriptures. Cain's sin in Genesis is punished with an explicit divine curse, while Onan's brings him death by natural causes for shirking his obligation to give life. On the other hand, and you know this better than I do, the Church repudiated Tertullian's Traducianism whereby the soul (and original sin with it) is transmitted through semen. St. Augustine was still trying to negotiate that idea through a form of *spiritual* Traducianism, but it was Creationism that gradually imposed itself, according to which God introduces the soul directly into the fetus at a given moment in its gestation.

St. Thomas used up precious stores of subtlety to explain how and why this was the case, and from that ensued a long discussion on the purely vegetative and sensory phases the fetus passes through and how only after these phases are completed is the fetus ready to receive intellectual spirit (I have just reread his wonderful meditations on this very question in both the *Summa* and the *Contra Gentiles*). I won't go on evoking the long debates undergone in order to determine at what phase of pregnancy definitive "humanization" occurs (what's more, I don't really know to what extent modern theology is still willing to consider this issue in Aristotelian terms of potentiality and actuality). I do want to say that at the very core of Christian theology lies the question of the threshold (a paper-thin threshold) beyond which what was a hypothesis, a germ — a dark articulation of life still tied to the mother body, a marvelous desire for the light, not unlike a seed deep in the earth struggling to flower — at a certain point is recognized as a *rational animal*, a *mortal*. Nonbelievers face the same problem; a human being is always born from this initial hypothesis. I am not a biologist (no more than I am a theologian) and don't feel equal to drawing any reasonable conclusions about where the threshold lies, or even if there is a threshold at all. No mathematical theory of catastrophe can tell us if there is a breaking point, a point of spontaneous explosion. We are perhaps condemned to know only that there is a process of which the miracle of the newborn baby is the final outcome. Determining when in the process we have the right to intrude, or when we no longer have the right, can be neither pinpointed nor discussed. And so, either the decision ought never to be made, or making it is a risk the mother must meet alone or before God or before the court of her own conscience and of humanity.

As I said, I'm not looking for some kind of pronouncement from you. I am asking for your comments on this impassioned theological debate that has gone on for centuries over a question that underlies our identification of ourselves as a part of a human society. Now that theology no longer measures itself against Aristotelian physics, but rather against the certainties (and uncertainties!) of modern experimental science, what is the current state of the theological debate? You know how such questions involve not only the abortion problem but a whole series of dramatic new issues such as genetic engineering, and how everyone, believer and nonbeliever, is debating bioethics today. Where does a modern theologian then stand in relation to classical creationism?

The definition of what life is, and where it begins, is a question that concerns our life. These are heavy questions, morally, intellectually, and emotionally — believe me — for me too.

Umberto Eco

Human Life Is Part
of God's Life

Dear Umberto Eco,

You are right to open your letter with a reminder that the aim of our epistolary exchange is to identify a common ground of discussion between laypeople and Catholics, and to approach issues about which there is no consensus, above all those issues that give rise to profound misunderstanding that then translates into political and social conflict. I agree, so long as we have the courage first to unmask the common misunderstandings that lie at the root of greater misunderstanding, making it easier for us then to confront the real differences. We must let ourselves become involved, show passion and sincerity, and be willing to "lay it all on the line" as we explore these central concerns. That is why I appreciate the clarification you offer on the subject of Life: the birth of a baby is "a marvelous thing, a natural miracle that we must accept."

Beginning from this, we recognize that the issue of Life (I'll get to your use of a capital L in a moment) is most certainly a critical point of contention, in particular as regards legislation on the voluntary termination of pregnancy. But here there is already a prime source of confusion. It is one thing to talk of human life and protecting human life from an ethical point of view; it's another to ask in what concrete way legislation can best defend those values in a given civil and political situation. Further confusion comes from what you've called "the banner of Life" that "when waved, can't but move the spirit." I suspect you'd agree with me that banners symbolize the big ideals of a general sort but aren't very useful for resolving complex questions in which there emerge conflicts of values within those big ideals. One needs then to reflect with caution, patience, sensitivity. Borders are always dangerous territory. As a boy, I remember walking in the mountains along the border in the Valle d'Aosta and suddenly wondering where exactly the border between the two nations was. I didn't understand how determining a border was humanly possible. The nations nonetheless did exist, and quite well defined.

A third source of misunderstanding is, as I perceive it, a confusion between the broad use — the "analogic" use (as the Scholastics would say; and I cite them with confidence because you assure me that you've just re-read parts of the *Summa* and the *Contra Gentiles*) — of the term "Life" and the restricted, proper use of the term "human life." The first sense embraces every living creature above the earth, on the earth, and under the earth, and also "Mother Earth" her-self with all her tremors, fecundity, and breath. In Milan our Ambrosian hymn for Thursday nights, referring to the first chapter of Genesis, sings:

> On the fourth day all that lives
> Thou hast brought, O God, from primordial
>> waters:
> The worm and fishes in the sea,
> The birds circling in the air.

47

But this broader concept of "Life" is not at issue here, however much its meaning can engender cultural, even religious, differences. The pressing ethical issue in this discussion regards "human life."

Even this point needs clarification. One sometimes imagines, or writes, that for Catholics human life represents the supreme value. This is, at the very least, imprecise, and doesn't correspond to what the Gospels tell us: "And do not fear those who kill the body but cannot kill the soul" (Matthew 10:28). The life that has supreme value in the Gospels is not the physical nor the psychic one (for these the Gospels use the Greek terms *bios* and *psyche*) but the divine life (*zoe*) communicated to man. These three terms are clearly distinguished in the New Testament, the first two subordinated to the third: "He who loves his life (*psyche*) loses it, and he who hates his own life (*psyche*) in this world will keep it for eternal life (*zoe*)" (John 12:25). So when we say "Life" with a capital letter, we should be referring first and foremost to that supreme and concrete Life and Being that is God himself. This is the Life that Jesus attributed to himself — "I am the way, and the truth, and the

48

Life" (John 14:6) — the Life in which every man and woman is called to participate. The supreme value in this world is man living the divine life.

This explains the Christian conception of the value of physical human life: the life of a person called upon to participate in the life of God himself. For Christians, respecting human life from its first manifestation is not an amorphous sentiment (you spoke of "personal disposition" and "intellectual persuasion"), but rather the fulfilling of a specific responsibility: that of a physical, living person whose dignity is not determined by a benevolent judgment on my part, or by a humanitarian impulse, but by a divine calling. It is something that is not only "me" or "mine" or even "inside of me," but before me.

On what does divine benevolence depend when I find myself facing a concrete life that I can label human? You've correctly noted that "everyone considers the newborn still attached to the umbilical cord to be a human being." But "how far back do we go from there?" Where does the "threshold" lie? You've also correctly recalled Thomas's subtle reflections on the distinct phases of the

development of life. I am neither a philosopher nor a biologist and wouldn't want to
intrude myself on such questions. But we all
know that we have a better understanding
today of the dynamics of human development
and a clearer sense of genetic determination
starting from a point that, at least in theory,
can be identified. From conception, in fact, a
new being is born. Here "new" means as distinct from the two elements that united to
form it. This being begins a process of development that will result in a baby, that "marvelous thing, a natural miracle that we must
accept." From its inception, this is the being
we are talking about. Identity has continuity.

Beyond these scientific and philosophical matters lies the fact that whatsoever is
open to so great a destiny — being called by
name by God himself — is worthy of enormous respect from the beginning. I wouldn't
want to invoke the generic right-to-life argument here, because it might be taken as impersonal or superficial. We are talking about real
responsibility toward that which is produced
by a great and personal love, responsibility
toward "someone." Being called upon and
loved, this someone already has a face, and is

the object of affection and attention. Every violation of this need of affection and attention can only result in conflict, profound suffering, and painful rending. We believe that everything should be done to keep this conflict and this rending from occurring. Such wounds heal with great difficulty, if ever. And it is above all the woman who will bear the scars, for the trust has been put in her primarily for that being which is most fragile and most noble in the world.

If this is the human and ethical problem, the civil problem is consequently how to help people and society at large to avert this rending? How does one give support to those who find themselves in an apparent, or real, conflict of conscience, so that they aren't destroyed by it?

You end by saying: "The definition of what life is, and where it begins, is a question that concerns our life." I agree completely — at least on the "what," on which I've already given my answer. The "where" can remain a mystery, but depends on the value placed on "what." Something of highest value warrants highest respect. Starting from here we could consider any specific case, a process which will always be daunting but never undertaken lightly.

One question remains. I have heavily emphasized that in the New Testament, it is not physical life itself that counts, but the life communicated by God. What could be the point of engaging in a dialogue on such a precise point of "revealed" doctrine? The first answer can be found in your expression of the anguish and trepidation felt by everyone considering the destiny of a human life, at whatever moment of its existence. There is a splendid metaphor that reveals in lay terms something common to both Catholics and laymen, that of the "face." Levinas spoke of it movingly as an irrefutable instance. I would rather cite the words, almost a testament, of Italo Mancini in one of his last books, *Tornino i volti* [Back to the Faces]: "Living in, loving, and sanctifying our world wasn't granted us by some impersonal theory of being, or by the facts of history, or by natural phenomena, but by the existence of those uncanny centers of otherness — the faces, faces to look at, to honor, to cherish."

Carlo Maria Martini

Men and Women — According to the Church

Dear Martini,

It's once again time for us to resume our conversation. And I must admit I'm a little sorry the editors have seen fit to make me go first every time; it makes me feel like a nag. Perhaps they've fallen victim to some banal cliché about philosophers specializing in the formulation of questions they don't know the answers to and pastors always having the right answer. Fortunately, in your previous letters, you demonstrate how complicated and agonized a pastor's reflections can be, thus disappointing those who might be expecting you to perform the function of oracle.

Before posing a question for which I have no answer, I'd like to put forth some premises.

When a religious authority of any persuasion pronounces upon principles of natural ethics, the layman should recognize that while he can agree or not, he has no reason to challenge the authority's right to make such a pronouncement — even if it is a criticism of the way the nonbeliever lives. Laymen have the right to challenge the position expressed by the religious authority only when it tends to force nonbelievers (or believers of another faith) to behave in a way forbidden by the laws of their state or religion, or prevents them from behaving in a way the laws of their state or their religion do allow.

I don't claim that the inverse right exists. A secular man does not have the right to criticize how a believer lives — except, again, if it runs counter to the laws of the state (the refusal to allow one's children to have a blood transfusion, for example) or limits the rights of those of a different faith. A religious perspective always proposes an ideal way of life, while a secular person sees an ideal life as the product of free choice, as long as that choice doesn't impinge on the free choice of others.

I believe no one has the right to judge the obligations different creeds impose on their followers. I have no right to object to the fact that Islam prohibits the consumption of alcohol; if I don't agree with this, I will not become Muslim. I can't see why secular people are scandalized by the Catholic Church's condemnation of divorce. If you want to be Catholic, don't get a divorce. If you want a divorce, become Protestant. You only have the right to protest if you are not Catholic and the Church wants to keep you from getting a divorce. I confess that homo-sexuals who want to be recognized by the Church and priests who want to get married exasperate me. I take off my shoes when I enter a mosque, and when I'm in Jerusalem I accept that in some buildings, on Saturday, the elevators run on automatic and stop at every floor. If I want to keep my shoes on or control the elevator, I go somewhere else. There are receptions (very secular affairs) for which a tuxedo is required, and it is up to me to decide if my reason for wanting to attend the event is compelling enough to warrant my stuffing myself into that irritating costume. I may decide to assert my freedom of choice by staying at home.

Now, if priests were to start a movement

asserting that, on nondoctrinal issues such as ecclesiastic celibacy, authority resides not with the Pope but with the community of followers in their own diocese, and if this movement attracted practitioners, I myself would refuse to sign a petition on their behalf. Not because I don't care about the issues, but because I am not part of their community and I have no right to stick my nose in concerns so exclusively ecclesiastic.

This said, it is a very different thing when a concerned secular person tries to understand why the Church approves or disapproves of certain things. If I invite an Orthodox Jew to dinner (there are many among my American colleagues who teach the philosophy of language) I take care (for reasons of courtesy) to ask in advance what he is willing to eat. But that doesn't stop me from questioning him on kosher cooking, in order to understand why they have to avoid foods that at first blush I would have thought even a rabbi could eat. So it seems legitimate for a layman to ask the Pope why the Church is against birth control, against abortion, against homosexuality. The Pope's reply to me, at least from the perspective of a strict interpretation of the precept *crescite et multiplicamini* [go forth and multiply], I admit makes sense. I could write an essay proposing an alternative hermeneutics, but until the Church agrees with my interpretation, it has the upper hand — the one with the scholiast's stylus in it.

And this is where my question comes in. I still have not managed to find persuasive reasons in Church doctrine for excluding women from the priesthood. I must repeat — I respect your autonomy regarding such delicate issues. If I were a woman who wanted to become a priest at all costs, I'd join the cult of Isis, and not try to force the hand of the Pope. But as an intellectual, as a (longtime) reader of the Scriptures, I harbor doubts on this question that I would like to dispel.

I see no scriptural rationale. From my reading of not only Leviticus but Exodus 29 and 30, I gather that the priesthood was entrusted to Aaron and his sons, not to their wives (we could even add, as Paul does in Hebrews, it was entrusted not to the order of Aaron but to that of Melchizedek — who apart from everything else enjoys historical and scriptural precedence; see Genesis 14 — though none of this affects our discussion).

But if I were a Protestant fundamentalist reading the Bible, I'd have to say with Leviticus that priests "shall shave neither head nor beard." I would then be utterly perplexed when I read Ezekiel 44:20, according to which priests must keep their hair short. What's more, according to both texts, no priest should go near dead bodies. And as a good fundamentalist I would expect a priest (even a Catholic priest) to follow either Leviticus, according to which priests can take wives, or Ezekiel, according to which they can marry only a virgin or the widow of another priest.

Even a believer will admit that the biblical authors adapted both chronicled events and disputes so they could be understood according to the customs and habits of the culture addressed. So if Joshua had pronounced "Halt O Earth!" or "Let the Newtonian law of universal gravity be suspended!" he'd have been thought insane. Jesus deemed it necessary to pay tribute to Caesar, given the political situation in the Mediterranean. This does not mean, however, that a European today should pay his taxes to the last descendent of the Hapsburgs, and if that taxpayer tried to deduct such a tribute from what he owed to his country, any savvy priest would (I hope) tell him he'd go to hell. The ninth commandment prohibits coveting another man's woman, but the Church has never questioned that, by synecdoche ["man" meaning "all people"], women likewise should not covet another woman's man.

It is obvious even to a believer that as God decided to incarnate the second figure of the Holy Trinity in Palestine in the epoch that he did, he was forced to incarnate that figure as a man, or else his word would not have carried any authority. I suspect you wouldn't disagree that if, by some inscrutable divine plan, Christ had been incarnated in Japan, he would have consecrated rice and saki, and the mystery of the Eucharist would still be what it is. If Christ had been incarnated some centuries later, when mountain prophetesses like Priscilla and Maximilla enjoyed popularity, he might have been incarnated in female form, maybe in the Roman civilization that held the vestal virgins in high regard. To deny this would mean affirming that woman is an impure being, which some societies in some periods have done, but surely not the current pontiff.

One could also apply symbolic reasoning:

The priest is the image of Christ, who was the ultimate priest, and Christ was male. The priesthood should thus be the prerogative of the male in order to preserve the potency of this symbol. But should Redemption follow the laws of iconography or of iconology?

Seeing as Christ beyond doubt sacrificed himself for men and women and, flouting custom, conferred the highest privileges upon his followers of the female gender, and seeing as the only human creature born without original sin was a woman, and seeing as it was before women and not men that Christ first appeared after his resurrection, are these not clear indications that — challenging the laws of his time, to the degree he could reasonably violate them — he wanted to demonstrate the equality of the sexes, if not before the law and historical usage at least in respect to Redemption? Mind you, I don't dare even venture into the vexed question of whether the word *Elohim*, which appears at the beginning of Genesis, is singular or plural, and might show grammatically that God has a gender (just as I'll take John Paul I's affirmation of God as a Mother to be only a figure of speech).

The symbolic argument doesn't satisfy

me. And I am likewise unconvinced by the archaic assertion that a woman secretes impurities at certain moments in her life (even if that view was held in the past — as if a menstruating woman or a woman giving birth is somehow more impure than a priest with AIDS).

When I find myself lost like this in matters of doctrine, I turn to the only person I trust, Thomas Aquinas. More than being *doctor angelicus*, Thomas was a man of extraordinarily good sense, who more than once confronted the question of whether the priesthood was an exclusively male prerogative. Limiting our discussion to the *Summa Theologica*, he sets forth this very question in II, 11, 2, where he wrangles with Paul's assertion (not even saints are perfect) that in the ecclesiastic assembly women should keep quiet and not be allowed to teach. But in Proverbs, Thomas finds *"Unigenitus fui coram matrem meam, ea docebat me"* [I was the sole joy of my mother; she taught me]. How does he get out of that? In accordance with the culture of his time (and how could he reject that?), the female sex should submit to the male sex, and women are not perfect in their wisdom.

In III, 31, 4, Thomas wonders if the substance of the body of Christ could have been taken from a female body (as you know, the Gnostic theories that were in circulation held that Christ passed through the body of Mary like water through a pipe, as if incidentally channeled, not touched by her body, not polluted by any of the *immunditia* that goes along with the physiology of childbirth). Thomas reminds us that if Christ had to be human, *convenientissimum tamen fuit ut de foemina carnem acciperet* [it was, however, most suitable that he took flesh from woman] because, as Augustine attested, "man's liberation must extend to both sexes." And yet he can't manage to divorce himself from his cultural context, and so allows that Christ *had* to be a man because the male sex is more noble.

But Thomas can move beyond his inescapable context. He doesn't deny that men are superior, and better adapted for wisdom than women, but he makes repeated efforts to figure out why women were accorded the gift of prophecy, and why abbesses were entrusted with the guidance and instruction of the soul — and he comes up with hairsplitting that is both elegant and reasonable. Yet he still doesn't seem convinced, and with his customary astuteness asks (pretending not to remember that he had already addressed this in I, 99, 2) if the male gender is the better, why, in that primordial state before original sin, did God also create woman? His answer is that it was right for both men and women to appear in the primordial state — not to guarantee the propagation of the species, since men were immortal and two sexes were not yet a necessary condition of survival, but because "Gender does not exist in the soul" (see *Supplementum* 39, 1, to which Thomas refers elsewhere, though the text was not by him). Indeed, for Thomas, gender was an accident produced during the last stages of gestation. It was right and necessary to create two sexes (and this becomes clearer in III, 4, in the *respondeo*) because mankind's origination comes out of an exceptional combination: the first man was conceived without man or woman, Eve was born of the man without the aid of a woman, and Christ was born of a woman without the participation of a man. But all other humans are born of a man and a woman. Apart from those three remarkable exceptions, this is the rule, and this is the divine plan.

In III, 67, 4, Thomas wonders if a woman can baptize, and easily dismisses the objections raised by tradition. It is Christ who performs baptism, but since (as Thomas gets from Paul in Colossians 3:11, although in fact it is stated more clearly in Galatians 3:28) *"in Christo non est masculus neque foemina"* [in Christ there is neither male nor female], if a man can perform a baptism, so can a woman. He then adds (the power of current opinion!) that *"caput mulieris est vir"* [the head (leader) of woman is man], so if there are men present a woman must not perform the baptism. But in his *ad primum* Thomas makes clear distinctions between what a woman is "not permitted" (according to custom) and that which she nonetheless "can" do (in terms of her rights). And in *ad tertium* he clarifies that if, on the carnal level, woman is fundamentally the passive principle and man the active, on the spiritual level this hierarchical distinction is no longer valid, because both men and women act through Christ.

Nonetheless, in *Supplementum* 39, 1 (which,

I recall, he didn't write himself) Thomas poses outright the question of whether a woman can enter the priesthood. To answer, he returns to the symbolic argument. The sacrament is also a sign, and its validity depends not only on the "thing" itself but also on the "sign of the thing." Inasmuch as no eminence attaches to the female gender, since women live in a state of subjugation, orders cannot be conferred upon a woman.

In answer to a question I can't remember the specifics of, Thomas also uses the *propter libidinem* [because of lust] argument: in other words, if a priest were female, her followers (male!) would be aroused by her. But a priest's followers are also women, so what of the young girls who might be excited at the sight of a handsome priest? (Think of the passage in Stendhal's *The Charterhouse of Parma* devoted to the phenomenon of unbridled passion stirred by Fabrizio del Dongo's sermons.) And the history of the University of Bologna includes the story of a certain Novella d'Andrea, who held a chair in the fourteenth century and was obliged to teach from behind a veil so as not to distract her students with her beauty. I choose to believe that Novella was not a vamp, but rather that her students tended toward a certain sophomoric lack of discipline. Therefore the story concerns the education of students, or followers, not the exclusion of women from the *gratia sermonis*.

In sum, it is my impression that not even Thomas knew why exactly the priesthood should be the exclusive prerogative of men, unless he assumed (as he did, and he couldn't have done otherwise, given the notions of his time) that men were of superior intelligence and dignity. But so far as I know this is not the Church's current position. Such a position would more closely reflect Chinese society, which, as we have recently learned to our horror, sanctions eliminating newborn girls in favor of male children.

Hence my confusion. What doctrinal reasons keep women out of the priesthood? If the reasoning is simply historical, based on incidental symbolism, because followers are accustomed to a male priest, then there is no reason to hurry the Church, which takes a long-term approach (though a date sometime before the Resurrection of the Body would be nice).

Clearly this is not a personal issue for me. I am simply curious. There are perhaps those in the "other half of Heaven" (as the Chinese say) who are genuinely eager to learn why.

Umberto Eco

The Church Does Not Fulfill Expectations, It Celebrates Mysteries

Dear Eco,

Yes, again it fell to you to initiate our dialogue. I don't suspect there are ideological reasons for designating who begins, but rather practical considerations. I had a number of commitments abroad during the month of September, and it's possible the editors found you easier to reach. For my part, I've been formulating a question to ask you and will hold it in reserve for the next round. It's a question I don't have an answer to, and I find no help even in the "oracular" function that you've noted is often mistakenly attributed to clergymen. At best, oracular powers are the province of prophets — but prophets are sadly rare in this day and age.

The question I have in mind for you concerns the layman's ethical foundation. I would so like to think that the men and women of this world have a clear ethical basis for their actions. And I'm convinced that many people do act honestly, at least in certain circumstances, without having a religious foundation to fall back on. Yet I cannot understand how they ultimately justify their actions.

I'll put this line of questioning aside for the moment and reserve it for the next letter — if indeed I get to go first — and turn now to the reflections you've proposed on the "hot topic" of women in the clergy. You state that as a layman you respect the position of religions on the principles and problems of natural ethics, but only if this does not impose behaviors on a nonbeliever or on believers of another faith that are prohibited by the laws of the state. I am in complete agreement with you. Any external imposition of principles or religious behavior on the nonconsenting violates freedom of conscience. I'll go even further and say that when such restraints took place in the past, in cultural circumstances different from those of today and for reasons that no longer apply, the religious body should rightly make amends.

This is the courageous position taken by John Paul II in his letter celebrating the year 2000, entitled *The Approach of the Third Millennium*, in which he says: "Another painful chapter which the children of the Church cannot revisit without a spirit of repentance is the acquiescence, during certain centuries in particular, to *methods of intolerance and even of violence* in the service of the truth. . . . It is true that to judge history correctly one must give attentive consideration to the cultural conditions of the moment. . . . But extenuating circumstances do not exonerate the Church from its obligation to feel deep regret for the weakness of many of its sons. . . . A lesson for the future emerges from these painful moments of the past, one that should compel every Christian to hold strictly to the golden rule set forth by the Church Court (*Dignitatis humanae* 1): 'Truth does not impose itself except by its own truth, which suffuses the mind in a simultaneous softness and strength' " (no. 35).

I would, however, like to make an important refinement to what you say regarding the "laws of the State." I agree with the general principle that a religious body should act in accordance with the laws of the State. Conversely, the lay community does not have the right to censor a believer's way of life as long as he remains within the framework of these laws. But I think (and I'm sure you'll agree) one cannot speak of the "laws of the State" as though they were absolute and immutable. Laws express the collective conscience of the majority of the citizens and such collective conscience is subject to free exchange of dialogue and alternative proposals, behind which lies (or can lie) profound ethical conviction. For this reason it is obvious that political movements and even religious bodies can try to democratically influence the tenor of laws they find do not correspond to an ethical standard that might indeed derive from religious practice but might also be shared by all citizens. The delicate game of democracy provides for a dialectic between opinions and beliefs in the hope that such exchange will expand the collective moral conscience that is the basis of orderly cohabitation.

It is in this spirit that I welcome your "hot

topic": the denial of the priesthood to women in the Catholic Church. You correctly position the question as that of a rational layman wishing to understand why the Church approves or disapproves of certain things, though in this case it is a theological problem, not an ethical one. We are concerned here with understanding why the Catholic Church — and along with it all of the Eastern Churches, meaning all the churches that claim a two-millennium-long tradition — continue to adhere to a specific cultural practice according to which women are excluded from the priesthood.

You say you have not yet been able to find persuasive doctrinal reasons to explain this, though you respect the Church's autonomy to decide such a delicate matter. You also express your confusion regarding the interpretation of the Scriptures, the so-called theological reasons, the symbolic reasons, right up to the biology tracts, before examining acutely certain passages of St. Thomas in which even this man of "extraordinary good sense" seems to indulge some rather inconsistent arguments.

Let's consider each of these points with

equanimity, although I will not attempt to engage in an involved discussion of the more subtle points — not because I dislike them or because I consider them superfluous, but because I fear that by doing so in this public context we'll lose our readers. I am already wondering if those readers not well acquainted with the Scriptures, and even less so with the writings of St. Thomas, have been able to follow all that you've said on the subject so far. But I am pleased that you have referred to these texts both because I am so familiar with them and because I hope it might encourage some curious readers to at least leaf through them.

Let's start with Scripture. You first bring up a general hermeneutic principle, according to which texts are not interpreted literally or from a fundamentalist point of view, but rather by considering the time and circumstances in which they were written. I completely agree with this principle; the exigencies of fundamentalism can only lead one racing down a blind alley. But I would object to your assertion that a fundamentalist would be disconcerted by the laws you cite regarding the hair and beards of priests.

You mention Ezekiel 44:20 and Leviticus (I think you are referring to Leviticus 19:27–28 and 21:5; see also Deuteronomy 14:1) to point out the contradiction that emerges from a literal interpretation of the texts: an unshorn beard for Leviticus and a short haircut for Ezekiel. To me (and to many other interpreters) it would appear that on this matter of detail (cited here only as an example) Ezekiel does not seek to contradict Leviticus. The latter is concerned with prohibiting certain rites of mourning probably of pagan origin (the text of 21:5 should be translated "do not shave the head, nor the sides of the beard, nor make incisions in the flesh" and Ezekiel is likely making reference to that same practice). I say this neither to defend fundamentalism nor to promote any particular hairstyle, but rather to demonstrate that it is not always easy to know what the Bible means in certain particular cases, nor to decide whether a given argument speaks to customs of the time or indicates a permanent condition of the people of God.

As concerns our present discussion, those who have looked to the Bible for arguments promoting the conferring of priesthood on woman have always run up against difficulty.

What can I say about arguments that might be considered "theological," such as your hypothesis that rice and saki might have been the elements of the Eucharist if "by some inscrutable divine plan, Christ had been incarnated in Japan"? Theology isn't the science of possibility or of "what might have happened if . . ." Theology can only begin with the actual, historical facts about revealed truth and attempt to understand them. For example, it is indisputable that Jesus Christ chose the twelve apostles, and beginning from that fact we must determine every other form of the Church's apostolate. This isn't a matter of trying to find a priori reasons, but rather accepting that God communicated in a specific way and through a specific history, whose particularity still determines what we do today.

I agree with you that symbolic reasoning, as it has been employed until now, is not convincing. You rightly note that Christ conferred high privileges on the women who followed him and appeared first to them after his

Resurrection. In opposition to the laws of his time, Christ offered distinct messages concerning the equality of the sexes. All of this is a given fact from which the Church must, in time, draw useful lessons, for we cannot think we have already taken all the strength we can from these operative principles. And any archaic biological argument has certainly long been obsolete.

This is also the reason why even St. Thomas, who was a man committed to doctrine as much as a man of enormous common sense, yet who could not move beyond the scientific conceptions nor intellectual habits of his time, was not able to propose arguments that would be persuasive to us today. I will not follow up on your subtle analysis of various passages of the *Summa*, not because I don't find it interesting but — again — because I fear our readers won't follow. Nonetheless your analysis demonstrates that St. Thomas was somewhat conflicted by diverging principles, and strained to find reasons for the Church's practice although aware himself that he was not entirely convincing. The principle *"sexus masculinus est nobilior quam feminus"* [the male sex is more noble than the female] (*Summa* III, 31,

4, *ad primum*) was a stumbling block, and on one hand he accepted it as evident in his own time, and on the other contrasted it with the privileges Christ and the Church accorded to women. To us, this principle belongs to the past and that is why any theological reasoning derived from it is invalid.

But, you will ask me, what does this all add up to? A very simple and very important thing: a Church practice that is profoundly rooted in tradition, and that has not really been deviated from through two millennia of history, is linked not solely to abstract or a priori reasoning but to something that maintains its own mystery. The fact that many of the reasons gathered over the centuries justifying why the priesthood is accorded only to men have lost their validity today, while the practice itself endures forcefully (think of the crisis provoked by the inverse practice, outside the Catholic Church, in the Anglican communion), tells us that we are up against not merely human reason but the Church's desire not to betray those redemptive events that gave rise to it and that derive not from human thought but from the very will of God.

Our pontiff is deeply concerned with

two important consequences of this. On one hand, the role and presence of women in all aspects of Church life and society must be realized, far beyond the degree to which it has been previously. On the other hand, our understanding of the nature of the priesthood and ordained ministers must be more profound than ever before. Permit me here to cite some very important words from Vatican II: "Our comprehension of things as well as received words is growing, either through the reflection and study of believers who mediate upon them with their hearts (see Luke 2:19 and 2:51), or through the experience conferred by a deeper knowledge of spiritual things, or through the teachings of those who by episcopal succession have received the power of truth. Over the course of centuries the Church has tended continuously toward the fulfillment of divine truth, until the words of God come to be realized through it" (*Dei Verbum* no. 8).

The Church recognizes therefore that it has not yet attained full understanding of the mysteries it lives and celebrates, but looks with confidence to a future that will permit it to live the fulfillment, not of the simple expectations or desires of humans, but of the promises of God himself. Along this journey, it will not deviate from the practice or example of Jesus Christ; for only by remaining completely faithful to him in exemplary fashion will it comprehend the implications of the liberation that, as St. Thomas reminds us (by citing St. Augustine), *in utroque sexu debuit apparere:* "It was ordained that the Son of God should receive his body from a woman . . . for thus was all human nature ennobled. This is why Augustine says, 'The liberation of man must manifest itself in both sexes' " (*Summa,* III, 31, 4).

Carlo Maria Martini

Where Does the Layman Find Illumination?

Dear Eco,

I can now pose to you the question I wanted to ask in my last letter, the one I told you about. It concerns the basic ethical foundation for a layman in the framework of the "postmodern." In more concrete terms: on what does he base the conviction and urgency of his moral behavior if, in creating an ethical system, he cannot call on *metaphysical* principles, transcendental values, or even universally valid *categorical imperatives*? Some readers complain that our discussions have been too difficult, so I'll put it even more simply: what guides the secular person who does not recognize a personal God, makes no appeal to an Absolute, yet claims and professes moral principles, principles so firmly held that this person would give his life for them, and uses those principles to determine what acts he will perform at any cost or will not perform under any circumstances? There are laws, certainly, but by what authority can they require something as great as the sacrifice of one's own life?

This is what I would like to reflect upon with you on this round of our exchange.

Of course, I'd like to think that all the men and women of this world, even those who do not believe in God, have distinct ethical foundations that lead them to act with righteousness so long as they adhere to them. I am also convinced that there are many people who do act with righteousness, at least in life's ordinary circumstances, without reference to a religious foundation for human existence. There have been those who, even though they didn't have a personal God, still sacrificed their lives rather than stray from their moral convictions. But I am unable somehow to understand what basic reason they would give for their behavior.

It is obvious that even a "lay" ethic can find and recognize the norms and values necessary for human coexistence. Indeed, that is how most modern legislation is born. But the establishment of a basis for these values that will not suffer from confusion and uncertainty, particularly in extreme cases — a basis that will not be mistaken simply for custom, convention, usage, functional or pragmatic behavior, even social necessity, but that assumes the weight of a true and right moral absolute — means not linking such a basis to mutable or negotiable principles.

This becomes even more important when we go beyond the realm of civil or penal law and enter the sphere of interpersonal relationships, of the responsibility each person has for the next, beyond written laws — the sphere of togetherness and giving freely.

By challenging the adequacy of a purely humanist basis, I do not mean to upset anyone's conscience. I am only trying to understand what happens within that conscience at the level of basic motivation, with the idea of fostering a more intensive communication between believers and nonbelievers on the subject of ethics.

Among the major religions there has already been much dialogue and debate about shared ethical principles. The aim of such dialogue is not only the elimination of religious conflict but also the advancement of mankind. Despite the historical and cultural differences in play, such a dialogue is possible because all religions invoke, though in different ways, some kind of transcendental Mystery as the basis for moral action. A series of general principles and behavioral norms can therefore be defined by which every religion can both identify itself and join in a common effort without having to renounce any of its own beliefs. Indeed, "religion can justify unambiguously why morality, norms, and ethical values must be binding *unconditionally* (and not simply when it's convenient) and hence *universally* (to all classes, ranks, and races). Man persists only insofar as he considers himself to be founded on the divine. It has become clear that only the unconditional can force unconditionally and only the absolute can bind us absolutely." (Hans Küng, *Project for a World Ethics*).

Would such a dialogue on ethics between believers and nonbelievers, in particular between Catholics and secular people, be possible? I've endeavored to understand through the communications of certain laymen some profound and somehow *absolute* reason behind their moral behavior. For example, I'm very interested in what underlies some people's impulse toward closeness and solidarity without having recourse to God the Father, Creator of All, and our brother Jesus Christ. My sense is that what they are more or less expressing is that the other is within us. He is a part of us, whether we love him, hate him, or are indifferent to him.

It would appear that this concept of the *other within* is considered by a segment of secular thought as the essential basis for notions of solidarity. I find this very striking, most especially when I see it in operation and leading to gestures of solidarity directed far away, toward the foreigner. I am struck also because when understood alongside St. Paul's reflections on the only Body of which we are all part (see Corinthians 12 and Romans 12) this position assumes a powerful realism, and can be read as a path into Christian faith. But I wonder whether the secular interpretation, lacking this fundamental justification, is sufficient, and whether it bears the force of inevitable conviction and is able to extend, for example, to the forgiving of one's enemies. Without the example and the word of Jesus Christ, who from the cross forgave his crucifiers, even religious traditions have difficulty with this last point. What can be said, then, about a secular ethical system?

I recognize that there are many people who behave with ethical correctness and sometimes perform acts of great altruism without having or without knowing if they have a transcendental basis for their efforts, and without referring either to a Lord Creator, or to the proclamation of the Kingdom of God with its ethical consequences, or to the death and resurrection of Jesus and the gift of the Holy Spirit, or to the promise of eternal life. It is from those realities that I derive the strength of my own ethical convictions, convictions that, in my weakness, I hope will always be the light and force of my actions. But without these or analogous principles, where does one find the light and the strength to act in the pursuit of good — not only when it's easy to do so, but also when the limits of human fortitude are being tested, when one is facing death? Why do altruism, sincerity, justice, respect for the other, and forgiveness of one's enemies represent good, and why are those values always to be preferred to their opposite? Why are they worth dying for? And how does one know with certainty in particular cases what is altruistic and what isn't? If there is not some ultimate, ever-valid justification for such attitudes, how can they possibly always prevail and win out? If even those who have strong arguments for ethical behavior struggle to comply, what becomes of those who operate with weak, uncertain, or wavering arguments?

It's difficult for me to see how an existence inspired by these standards (altruism, sincerity, justice, solidarity, forgiveness) can be sustained for long in any and every given circumstance when their absolute value is not founded on *metaphysical* principles or on a personal God.

It is very important to find a common ethical ground between laymen and believers, so that both can work for the betterment of mankind, for peace and justice. The appeal to human dignity clearly constitutes a principle that establishes a universal basis for thought and action: never to take advantage of another person, always and everywhere to respect the inviolability of the other, always to consider every person as an unusable and untouchable reality. Nonetheless, at a certain point one must ask what the ultimate justification for these principles is. What is human dignity based on if not the fact that every person is open to something higher and larger than himself? This is the only way human dignity will not be circumscribed by baser concerns, the only way to guarantee an inviolability that nothing can put into question.

I feel a great desire to reinforce everything that promotes community of action between believers and nonbelievers toward the advancement of mankind. I am also aware, however, that sooner or later, without an accord on fundamental principles, something will be triggered that reveals a fundamental divergence when we come to extreme cases or cutting-edge questions. Solidarity becomes more difficult, and conflicting ethical judgments concerning central issues of life and death begin to emerge.

So what do we do? Proceed together with modesty and humility on those points about which we agree, hoping that opposing motives and conflicts will simply never arise?

Or do we work together to try and deepen the logic of general agreement on subjects such as justice, peace, human dignity, in order to arrive at those unspoken principles that lie behind our daily decisions, and that reveal either a basic disagreement, which will stand as it is, or perhaps the possibility of moving beyond skepticism and agnosticism toward a "Mystery" we can all put our faith in because from it is born the chance to build a more humane world?

It is on this gripping question that I would like to know your thoughts. Discussion of specific ethical issues always brings one back to questions about what underlies them. So it does seem worthwhile to investigate these topics, to shed a little light on what each of us thinks and to better understand the other's point of view.

Carlo Maria Martini

Ethics Are Born in the Presence of the Other

Dear Martini,

Your letter has lifted me out of one awkward position only to deposit me in another equally as awkward. Until now, I have been the one (not by choice) to open the dialogue; and whoever speaks first in such a dialogue inevitably formulates his questions in anticipation of the other's response. Hence my feeling that I was cast in the role of inquisitor. That being so, I have very much appreciated the decisiveness and humility with which, all three times, you disabused our readers of the myth that Jesuits always answer a question with another question.

Now, however, I find that addressing your question is awkward too. Had I had a secular education, my answer might be worth something. But I was heavily influenced by Catholicism up until (to mark the precise moment of my fall) I was twenty-two years old. Secularism was not a legacy I passively absorbed, but rather the fruit of a long, slow, and painful process. And I am still unsure whether some of my moral convictions are not somehow dependent on the religious teaching that had such influence on me at the beginning. Now, at my advanced age, I have seen (in a foreign Catholic university that hires secular professors, but then asks them to manifest full religious observance) my colleagues draw near the sacrament without believing in the literal "presence" — and therefore without even having confessed. With a shudder I still felt, after so many years, the horror of the sacrilege.

Nonetheless, I do believe I can say on what foundations my secular "religiosity" is based today, because I firmly hold that there are forms of religiosity, and therefore a sense of the sacred, of the finite, of investigation and expectation, of a communion with something greater — even in the absence of faith in a personal and provident divinity. But I understand from your letter that this is something you know as well as I do. Indeed, you are asking what is in these ethical systems that is binding, compelling, and unrenounceable.

I would like to put things in a larger context. Certain ethical problems become more clear to me when I reflect on certain semantic questions — and it doesn't matter if some find our discussion too difficult: they have doubtless been encouraged to think in simplistic terms by mass-media "revelations" which are predictable by definition. Let them learn to think hard, for neither the mystery itself nor the evidence is easy.

What is at issue is knowing whether there is a "universal semantic," elementary notions common to everyone in the human race that can be expressed in all languages. Not a simple matter when one understands that many cultures don't recognize notions which seem evident to us, such as, for example, the idea of substance endowed with certain properties (when we say "the apple is red"), or the idea of identity (a=a). I am nonetheless convinced that notions common to all cultures exist, and that they all refer to the position of our bodies in space.

We are animals of erect stature, for whom it is painful to remain upside down for long. We therefore have a common notion of up and down, and tend to privilege the former over the latter. We likewise have a notion of right and left, of immobility or motion, sitting up or lying down, crawling or jumping, of being awake or asleep. Because we have arms and legs, we know what it means to hit against something hard, to reach into something soft or liquid, to squash, to shake, to batter, to kick, maybe even to dance. The list could go on and include seeing, hearing, eating and drinking, swallowing or spitting. Most certainly every man has a notion of what it means to perceive, to remember, to feel desire, fear, sadness or relief, pleasure or pain, and to emit sounds that express those sensations. As a result (and here we enter the realm of rights), we have universal conceptions of constraint: we don't want someone to keep us from talking, seeing, listening, sleeping, swallowing or spitting, from going where we want. We suffer if someone binds us or segregates us, strikes us, hurts or kills us, subjects us to a physical or psychic torture that diminishes or destroys our ability to think.

92

Up to this point, I've only presented a sort of bestial and solitary Adam, who does not yet know what sex is, or the pleasure of dialogue, or parental love, or the pain of losing someone you care about. And yet, even in this phase, at least for us (if not for him or her), this semantic has become the basis for an ethical system: we should, above all, respect the physical rights of others, including the right to speak and think. If our own kind had respected these rights, we would never have had the Massacre of the Innocents, Christians fed to the lions, the Night of St. Bartholomew, the burning of heretics, extermination camps, censorship, children working in the mines, atrocities in Bosnia.

But how is it possible, given this instinctive repertory of universal perceptions, that the beast (or beastess) that I've depicted here — all astonishment and ferocity — manages to comprehend not only that he wants to do certain things and not have other things done to him, but also that he shouldn't do to others what he doesn't want done to himself? Because, fortunately, Eden was quickly populated, and the ethical dimension comes into play when the other arrives on the scene. Every law, moral or civil, regulates interpersonal relationships, including relationships with those who impose the law.

You too attribute to our virtuous secular man the belief that the other is in us. This is not a vague sentimental propensity, but rather a basic condition. As we are taught by the most secular of the social sciences, it is the other, his gaze, that defines us and determines us. Just as we couldn't live without eating or sleeping, we cannot understand who we are without the gaze and reaction of the other. Even those who kill, rape, rob, and violate do so in exceptional moments, and the rest of the time beg love, respect, praise from others. And even from those they humiliate, they ask recognition in the form of fear and submission. Without any such recognition, the newborn abandoned in the forest will not become a human (or else, like Tarzan, he will look for the other in the face of an ape). We might die or go insane if we lived in a community in which everyone had systematically decided never to look at us and to behave as if we didn't exist.

Why then is it that certain cultures condone, or have condoned in the past, murder, cannibalism, the humiliation of another human body? Simply because those cultures restrict their concept of the "other" to those within their own tribal community (or ethnicity) and think of the "barbarians" (the outsider) as inhuman. Not even the Crusaders thought of the infidels as brethren to love beyond measure. The recognition of the role the other plays, the necessity to respect in him those very needs we could not ourselves live without fulfilling, is the fruit of millennial progress. Even the Christian commandment to love was enunciated, and accepted with difficulty, only when the time was ripe.

You ask if consciousness of the other's importance provides me with an absolute base, an unshakable foundation for ethical behavior. I could reply by saying that even what you define as an absolute foundation still has not kept many believers from sinning while being conscious of sin, and our discussion might end there. The temptation to evil lurks even in those who have a solid and revealed notion of good. But I prefer to offer two personal anecdotes that have given me much cause for reflection.

The first concerns a writer who calls

himself Catholic — even if *sui generis* — whose name I won't reveal because he told me the story in a private conversation and I am not a tattletale. This was during the time of John XXIII and my elderly friend was enthusiastically extolling the Pope's virtues, saying (with evident paradoxical intent), "Pope John must be an atheist. Only someone who doesn't believe in God could love his own kind so much!" Like all paradoxes, this one contained a germ of truth: without considering the atheist (a figure whose psychology eludes me because, like Kant, I don't see how one can possibly not believe in God, can maintain that it is impossible to prove his existence, and yet also firmly believe in the nonexistence of God, maintaining that this can be proved), it seems evident to me that someone who has never experienced transcendence, or who has lost it, can make sense of his own life and death, can be comforted simply by his love for others, by his attempt to guarantee someone else a livable life even after he himself has disappeared. Certainly, there are those nonbelievers who are not at all worried about giving meaning to their own death. There are also those who claim to be faithful but would be willing to rip the heart from a living baby in order to preserve their own lives. The power of an ethical system is judged by the behavior of the saints, not of the benighted *cuius deus venter est* [whose god is the belly].

Which brings me to the second anecdote. I was still a young Catholic, sixteen years old, and I became involved in a verbal duel with a man I knew, older than I, who had been labeled a "communist" in the sense that this term had in the fearsome fifties. As I got worked up, I posed a decisive question: How could he, a nonbeliever, make meaning out of something as otherwise meaningless as his own death? His answer was: "By asking before I die for a public funeral, so that, though I am no longer, I have left an example to others." I suspect that you too can admire this profound faith in the continuity of life, the absolute sense of duty animating his response. This is the sense of meaning that has led many nonbelievers to die under torture rather than betray friends, and led others to expose themselves to plagues so that they could cure the suffering of others. Sometimes it is the only thing that drives a philosopher to philosophize, a writer to write: to leave a message in

a bottle, because in some way what one
believes or what one finds beautiful can be
believed or seen as beautiful by those who
come after.

Is this feeling strong enough to justify an
ethic as determined and inflexible, as solidly
based, as that of people who believe in
revealed morality, in the survival of the soul,
in reward and retribution? I have tried to base
secular ethical principles on the natural fact
(and therefore, for you, the result of a divine
plan) of our corporeality, and on the notion
that only the presence of the other makes us
understand instinctively that we have a soul
(or something that functions as such). What I
have defined as a secular ethic is at its root a
natural ethic, one that not even a believer
denies. Isn't natural instinct, carried to proper
maturation and self-awareness, a basis that
offers sufficient guarantee? We can of course
think that there might not be sufficient impe-
tus for virtue: a nonbeliever might think the
evil he is doing in secret goes unseen. But keep
in mind, if the nonbeliever thinks that no one
is watching him from on high, he thereby also
knows — for this very reason — that no one
will forgive him. Knowing he's done evil, his

solitude will be infinite, his death desperate. This person is more likely than the believer to attempt to purify himself through public confession; he will ask forgiveness from others. He knows his predicament from the core of his being, and so he also knows in advance that he must forgive others. Otherwise how does one explain that nonbelievers are also capable of feeling remorse?

I'm not in favor of instituting a clear-cut opposition between believers of a transcendental God and those who don't believe in any notion of a superior being. Let's not forget that *Ethics* is precisely the title of Spinoza's major work and that it opens with the definition of God as his own creation. This Spinozian divinity, as we well know, is neither transcendent nor personal. Yet even the vision of a great and unique cosmic Substance into which we will one day be reabsorbed can generate a vision of tolerance and of benevolence, precisely because we are all invested in maintaining the equilibrium and harmony of the only Substance. We think it impossible that this Substance is not somehow enriched or deformed by what we have done through the millennia — that is why we care. So I'll dare suggest (not a metaphysical hypothesis, but only a timid concession to the hope that never abandons us) that the question of some kind of life after death can be reproposed even from this perspective. Today's electronic universe teaches us that message sequences can be transmitted from one physical apparatus to another without losing their unique characteristics, and seem even to survive as purely immaterial algorithms from the instant they leave one physical apparatus to when they reach the other. Who knows if death, rather than being an implosion, may be an explosion — the impression, from somewhere between the vortices of the universe, of the software (what others might call soul) created by our living, made up of memories and regrets, and thus our implacable suffering, or sense of peace for a duty fulfilled, and love.

You say that without the example and word of Christ, secular ethics lacks the basic justification that would endow it with the strength of ineluctable conviction. Why are you taking away from the layman the right to avail himself of the example of a forgiving Christ? Can you, Carlo Maria Martini, for the sake of our discussion and the confrontation

100

in which you believe, try to think for a
moment that there is no God: that man
appeared on Earth through a clumsy accident,
consigned to mortality but also condemned to
be aware of this, and that therefore he is the
most imperfect among all the animals (and
permit me my gloomy Leopardian tone for
this hypothesis). This man, to find the
courage to face death, would out of necessity
become a religious creature and aspire to construct narratives capable of providing an
explanation and a model, an exemplary
image. And of those that he can dream up —
some illuminating, some terrible, some
pathetically self-consolatory — in the fullness of time, he has at a given moment the
religious and moral and poetic strength to
conceive the model of Christ, of universal
love, of forgiveness of one's enemies, of life
offered in terrible sacrifice for the salvation of
the other. If I were a traveler from a distant
galaxy and found myself before a species that
knew how to construct such a model, I would
be captivated, I would admire all this theo-
gonic energy, and I would judge this wicked
and miserable species, this species that committed so many horrors, redeemed solely

101

because it had succeeded in desiring and believing that all of it was the Truth.

Abandon my hypothesis; leave it for others. But admit that even if Christ were only a character in a great story, the fact that this story could have been imagined and desired by featherless bipeds who only knew that they didn't know, would be as miraculous (miraculously mysterious) as the fact that the son of a real God was really incarnated. This natural and earthly mystery would never stop stirring and softening the hearts of nonbelievers.

This is why I believe that on fundamental points a natural ethic — worthy of respect for the deep religiosity that animates it — can match the principles of an ethic founded on faith in transcendence, which cannot but recognize that the natural principles were carved into our hearts in anticipation of salvation. If there are still — and of course there are — smaller matters that don't harmonize, the same happens in the confrontation of different religions. And in the conflicts of faith Kindness and Prudence should prevail.

Umberto Eco